Presents.

DEPRESSION

COPYRIGHT © 2019. ALL RIGHTS RESERVED.

No part of this publication may be reproduced, distributed, or transmitted in any form or by any means, including photocopying, recording, or other electronic or mechanical methods, or by any information storage and retrieval system without the prior written permission of the publisher, except in the case of very brief quotations embodied in critical reviews and certain other noncommercial uses permitted by copyright law.

INTRODUCTION

CHAPTER 1
HISTORY OF DEPRESSION

CHAPTER 2
DEPRESSION: FACTS AND STATISTICS

CHAPTER 3
WHAT IS THE EXACT DEFINITION OF DEPRESSION?

CHAPTER 4
TYPES OF DEPRESSION

CHAPTER 5
SIGNS OF DEPRESSION

CHAPTER 6
CAUSES OF DEPRESSION

CHAPTER 7
63 IDEAS TO GET RID OF DEPRESSION

CONCLUSION

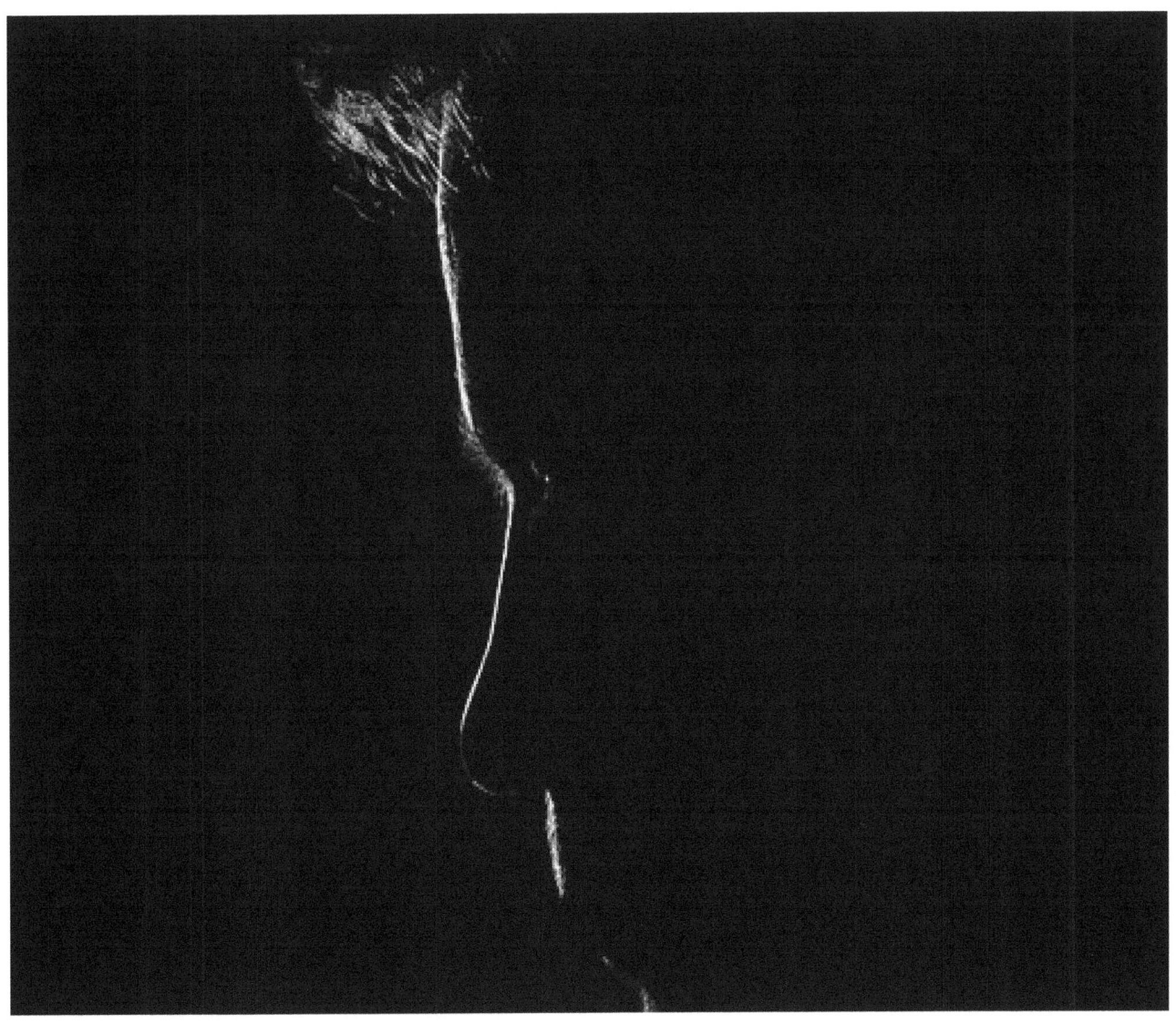

Every man has his secret sorrows which the world knows not; and often times we call a man cold when he is only sad.

Henry Wadsworth Longfellow

INTRODUCTION

Almost 10% of our population over the age of 18 suffers with some form of depression disorder. Living in a developed country like our own seems to put us more at risk as 15% on average of the population of developed countries have it. This may lead some to deduce that there may be something in our "development" that creates a depressive response.

In any case, signs of depression may include insomnia, oversleeping, lack of interest, indifference, unusual weight loss or gain, fatigue, tiredness, lack of mental focus, apathy, sadness, anxiety, and feelings of hopelessness, inadequacy, and worthlessness. Physical effects can include cardiovascular disease, hormonal imbalances, and even more serious conditions and diseases.

With all this being said, in many cases, depression begins with the suppression of feelings. This means that feelings that are uncomfortable or painful like worthlessness, inadequacy, betrayal, loneliness, insecurity, loss, helplessness, failure, rejection and abandonment are pushed down into the subconscious and hidden.

The hallmark of energy is movement. Emotions are a form of energy that must move. They should be felt, no matter how uncomfortable, and allowed into consciousness in order to be discharged. This would allow the feelings to cycle properly and be released.

Suppression occurs when we knowingly ignore or push down uncomfortable feelings into the subconscious and stop their cycling.

When we continue to "push down" these emotions when they are trying to be released from the subconscious, it is called repression. The more we repress, the stronger these emotions become. This can often lead to the addictions to drugs, medications, food, and even activity, that provides more energy to keep these unresolved feelings held hidden. Making spiritual progress is severely hampered by suppression and repression. Our ability to feel is also compromised. There are effective ways to work through these emotions. Avoidance will only make life more difficult and miserable.

Let's be honest, your road to recovery has to begin with courage. Take the first step, you're worth it.

CHAPTER 1
HISTORY OF DEPRESSION

We've discussed Depression from a number of different angles, but we've yet to discover its history. Not so much where did it come from. One may be sure that mental illness generally has been a thorn in the side of humanity ever since man first set foot on earth, and even animals are diagnosed with the condition.

But who first became aware of it? Homer's 'Iliad' gives us a glimpse, when Ajax rescues Achilles, only to see Achilles' armour given away to Odysseus. He flies into a terrible rage and slaughters a flock of sheep in the belief that they're the enemy. After coming to his senses, he's so overcome with shame, that he kills himself.

Here, though, we see a mental disorder directly attributable to two outside acts. The armour he considers that he's won is given away to another, which infuriates him to the point where he becomes unbalanced. Then he has a go at the poor old sheep, at which time he's probably hallucinating. When sanity re-visits him, the shame he feels forces him into suicide.

A different time, different situation to that which we're used, but the outcome's the same. A psychotic outburst, the likes of which we've seen down the centuries to the present day.

Hippocrates, in 400 B.C.E. used the names 'Mania' and 'Melancholia' to describe certain conditions of the mind that he noticed himself. Aulus Cornelius Celsus, in 30 C.E., wrote his treatise "De Re Medicana," in which he described melancholia and even mentioned depression. He was of the opinion that it was caused by black bile.

The next landmark hypothesis seems to have been put forward by Maimonides in the twelfth century. Among many other accomplishments, he was a Jewish physician who was the first to see the possibility that Melancholia was a discrete disease entity, in other words rather than seeing pain as the direct result of trauma or physical injury, he considered that it fundamentally changed the entire nervous system.

As we've seen with Celsus and his black bile theory, depression and similar mental disorders were considered physical in origin, so Maimonides certainly took a step in the right direction.

It seems that the diagnostic wheels of mental illness ground slow indeed, for it wasn't until 1686 that a doctor named Bonet described an illness he named Maniaco Melancholicus, and two hundred years after that, the doctor Jules Falret called the condition of alternating moods of mania and depression, 'folie circulaire.'

However, in 1899, the German psychiatrist, Emil Kraepelin, explained the illness as 'manic - depressive psychosis.' He freely admitted that he'd stood on the shoulders of the doctors who'd gone before him. The methods and criteria he used for his diagnosis of the condition are very similar to those used today.

He was born on the 15th. February 1856 and died on the 7th. October 1926. He considered psychiatric illness to be both a biological and genetic problem. He's the first to have divided psychosis into two forms; Manic Depression, which we know now as being both major depression and bi-polar disorder, and Dementia Praecox. It should be pointed out, though, that Arnold Pick first used this Latin description in 1891.

However, in 1896, Kraeplin first brought the illness to the attention of the public when he gave a detailed description of it. The condition is now known to us as Schizophrenia. When you look back over the centuries that have gone before, and consider the suffering endured by so many people who had no idea what was wrong with them, any more than did the doctors, it makes you very glad to live in the twenty first century, warts and all.

CHAPTER 2

DEPRESSION: FACTS AND STATISTICS

Depression is very serious.

It is the main cause for suicide.

People are killing themselves by the thousands, because of this dangerous disease.

In this chapter, we will see how depression is increasing alarmingly worldwide.

According to figures released by the World Health Organization (WHO) for 2010: Globally, more than 350 million people of all ages suffer from depression, or about 5% of the world population. Even worse, Depression is the leading cause of disability worldwide, and is a major contributor to the global burden of disease.

The WHO also reports that suicide rates have increased 60 percent over the past 50 years, most strikingly in the developing world, and that by 2020 depression will be the second most prevalent medical condition in the world.

Studies strongly prove that depression is not restricted to any specific race or certain individuals.

All individuals are vulnerable to depression!!!

As a matter of fact, even intelligent and creative persons experienced depression, and the list includes:

Ernest Hemmingway, Ludwig van Beethoven, Sylvia Plath, Edgar Allan Poe, Mark Twain, Georgia O'Keefe, John Lennon, Vincent van Gogh, and F. Scott Fitzgerald.

The latest victim of depression was the late Robin Williams.

One clear indication of the rapid increase of depression was evident in the 2013 study of global consumption of antidepressants, by the Guardian. The study focused on 25 countries, and it noticed that since the year 2000, every single covered country has increased its consumption of antidepressants. Some data show that the US consumption of antidepressants increased 400% between 1988 and 2008 (CDC)

A - Some Depression Statistics By Country

1 - USA:

According to the Centers for Disease Control and Prevention (CDC), in 2012, major depression is the leading cause of disability for Americans between the ages of 15 and 44.

- CDC, 2012: While major depressive disorder can develop at any age, the median age at onset is 32.5.

-In 1991 depression rates for American adults stood at 3.33% of the population, according to The American Journal of Psychiatry. In 2011, CDC numbers show that it reached approximately 10 percent of Americans ages 18 and over in a given year, or more than 24 million people.

-Depression is involved in more than two - thirds of the 39,000 suicides that occur in the United States every year. For every two homicides, there are three suicides.

-CDC: Suicide is the fourth leading cause of death for adults between the ages of 15 and 64 years in the United States. Currently, suicide is the 10th leading cause of death in the United States, 2011. (Last available data).

-According to the National Institute of Mental Health (NIMH), which is the largest scientific organization for mental health issues, women are 70 % more likely than men to experience depression during the course of their lifetimes.

-According to CDC: More Americans suffer from depression than coronary heart disease (17 million), cancer (12 million) and HIV/AIDS (1 million).

-About 15 percent of the population will suffer from clinical depression at some time during their lifetime. Thirty percent of all clinically depressed patients attempt suicide; half of them ultimately die by suicide. CDC

2 - Australia:

Australia has the second highest antidepressants consumption in the world, only after Iceland.

According to the National Survey of Mental Health and Wellbeing: Suicide is the biggest killer of young Australians and accounts for the deaths of more young people than car accidents. Breakdown: 324 Australians (10.5 per 100,000) aged 15 - 24 dying by suicide in 2012. This compares to 198 (6.4 per 100,000) who died in car accidents (the second highest killer)

-According to Australian Bureau of Statistics, 2008: One million people in Australia, suffer from depression.

3 -Canada:

Canada has the third highest consumption rate of antidepressants in the world.

-According to latest figures released by the Canadian Mental Health Association:

-Suicide accounts for 24% of all deaths among 15 - 24 year - olds and 16% among 25 - 44 year - olds.

-Suicide is one of the leading causes of death in both men and women from adolescence to middle age.

-The mortality rate due to suicide among men is four times the rate among women.

- Today, approximately 5% of male youth and 12% of female youth, age 12 to 19, have experienced a major depressive episode.

- The total number of 12 - 19 year - olds in Canada at risk for developing depression is a staggering 3.2 million.

4 - Japan:

-According to the Organization for Economic Cooperation and Development OECD, Japan has one of the highest suicide rates, at 21 people per 100,000, compared to the United States' rate of 12 per 100,000. In 2010, 31,690 people in Japan killed themselves.

-According to her book "Depression in Japan," anthropologist Junko Kitanaka writes that the number of diagnoses of depression in that country more than doubled between 1999 and 2008.

5 - China:

Although China does not publish official statistics on mental health, most evidence suggests that its depression rate is on the rise.

China may be home to more than 30 million depression patients, or 3% - 5% of the total population, according to a 2012 report by the market data company Research and Markets. The report indicates that the country's antidepressant market is booming. About £326m of the drugs were sold in 2012 - a small portion of China's pharmaceuticals market as a whole, but growing quickly, with a 22.6% increase on 2011.

6 - India:

The National Crime Records Bureau (NCRB) statistics reveal that a total of 1,35,445 people in India committed suicide in 2012 which amounts to an average of 15 suicides an hour or 371 suicides daily. Tamil Nadu state ranked the first on the suicide index, and Maharashtra ranked second.

-Suicide rate for Tamil Nadu was 25 per 100,000, in2012, which is among the highest in the world.

-Ironically, the top five States with the highest rates of suicides are from the South, which are among the richest states of India.

- According to a study conducted by the global health agency, World Health Organization (WHO), chances of an individual developing depression during the lifetime is nine percent in India.

-As per WHO, the average age of depression in India is 31.9 years.

B - Who Is Most Vulnerable to Depression?

According to a study by NIMH the following groups are more likely to develop major depression:

- Persons 45 - 64 years of age

- Blacks, Hispanics, non - Hispanic persons of other races or multiple races

- Women

- Those previously married

- Persons with less than a high school education

- Individuals unable to work or unemployed

- Persons without health insurance coverage

- Married women are more likely to be depressed than unmarried women.

- Married men are less likely to be depressed than unmarried men.

- Unhappily married women are three times more likely to be depressed than unhappily married men.

- Highest suicide rate among Americans is in white men who are 85 or older.

- Many studies have found that being divorced, separated, or widowed is closely linked to depression. The loss of a marriage may lead to depression, or depression may lead to loss of a marriage.

A 2000/2001 study published in the journal Depression and Anxiety that analyzed depression statistics from the Canadian National Population Health Survey found that major depression doubled a person's chance of becoming divorced or separated.

- NIMH also found that depression can be the result of the following:

- 50% to 75% of those who have an eating disorder.

- 25% of those who have cancer

- More than 40% of those with post - traumatic stress disorder

- 27% of those with substance abuse problems

- 33% of those who've had a heart attack

- 50% of those with Parkinson's disease

C - Conclusions

We used to have many stereotypes about depression.

- We thought it was confined to old people.
- We assumed it to be only for the poor.
- We thought money would make it disappear.
- We believed it affected the unintelligent person.

Those statistics gathered from around the world showed us that we were Wrong.
We better get rid of those myths about depression.

Six months ago, I lost a close friend because of his suicide.

Ritty was his name. He was from Holland.

What was striking to me that he never showed any indication of his suicide.

Depression can come faster than we may think.

It is no longer a personal dilemma.

It is penetrating every country, without Détente.

The statistics here may be alarming and frightening. But they are good for us.

We don't want to be Ostriches burying their heads in the sand when they're scared or threatened.

We need a wake up call, before it is too late.

Too late for what?

For a solution, salvation or a treatment.

CHAPTER 3
WHAT IS THE EXACT DEFINITION OF DEPRESSION?

How would you define depression? That must surely be a million dollar question because it is virtually impossible to define depression with only a few words. In fact, to define it properly would require several books. Having said that, most people nowadays do have a basic understanding as to what is meant by the term 'depression', but none the less, let's just go ahead and say that depression is a state of mind which usually follows an event which has given rise to feelings of sadness and/or resentment. However, in the case of depression, this depressive state of mind tends to be out of proportion to the reason which caused it.

How else can we define depression?

o It is a condition which more than 100 million people from around the globe suffer from on a daily basis

o It is a mental condition which is becoming ever more prevalent in society

o It is a condition which is affecting more and more children regularly

o It is a condition which can be treated but often left untreated

Even though there are so many different forms of treatment, some more successful than others, and some with fewer side effects than others, doctors, psychiatrists, and psychologists have yet to pinpoint the exact cause of depression. However, it is known that the following factors may contribute:

o Genetics

o Medication

o Chemical imbalances in the brain

o Long-term negative mental attitude

o Immediate environment

o Established undesirable behavioral patterns

o Relationship problems

o Childhood abuse

o Sexual abuse

While these are by no means the only factors which could contribute towards a person becoming depressive, they are certainly amongst the most common factors. However, the vast majority of the medical professions are in agreement that depression is for the most part a result of several factors rather than a single factor. In other words, while a person may be capable of dealing with something, such as having been abused as a child, when another contributing factor is added, depression can often result.

Interestingly enough, there is still a phenomenal amount of research being done in which scientists are now investigating the role of neurotransmitters in the brain. These are essentially chemicals which occur naturally in the brain and which are responsible for various communication processes. The three chemicals which have been attracted the most attention are:

1. Serotonin

2. Dopamine

3. Norepinephine

Generally speaking, these chemicals are responsible for the "feel good" feeling, and this is why the vast majority of prescription antidepressants focus on altering the quantity of these chemicals in the brain. Additionally, certain antidepressants work by preventing the body of depleting these chemicals. By preventing depletion or by increasing production, it is possible to promote a feeling of well being and as such, it is possible to alleviate the symptoms of depression.

However, by their very nature, many of the drugs which are used to achieve these results are known to cause dependency.

CHAPTER 4
TYPES OF DEPRESSION

Depression is complex. It can linger and grow for months or even years before being detected . Studies have shown that millions of Americans will suffer some form of depressive disorder this year. Unfortunately fewer than 1/3 of these people will look for help. Often the sufferers don't even know they're sick. Every day stress is common in the modern world. It's more difficult to navigate the obstacles in life. Many families are surviving week to week. Trouble in the economy has made it more difficult than ever to keep a good job. Stress leads to depressive feelings. There are many different types of depression. Some of the labels mean the same thing. There is mental, medical, clinical and manic depressive disorder. There is also the fact that it gets severe enough to allude to the final stages of the disease. Depressive disorder can result from a variety of causes. One of these is simple biology, brain chemistry issues. DNA also carries it. Those with family histories of the disorder are at risk.

Psychology Information Online provides information on the following depressive disorders:

* Major Depression - This is the most serious type, in terms of number of symptoms and severity of symptoms, but there are significant individual differences in the symptoms and severity. You do not need to feel suicidal to have a major case, and you do not need to have a history of hospitalizations either, although both of these factors are present in some people with major depressive symptoms.

* Dysthymic Disorder - This refers to a low to moderate level that persists for at least two years, and often longer. While the symptoms are not as severe as the major version, they are more enduring and resistant to treatment. Some people with dysthymia develop a major case at some time during the course of their disorder.

* Unspecified - This category is used to help researchers who are studying other specific types, and do not want their data confounded with marginal diagnoses. It includes people with a serious case, but not quite severe enough to have a diagnosis of a major form. It also includes people with chronic, moderate, which has not been present long enough for a diagnosis of a Dysthymic disorder. (You get the idea!)

* Adjustment Disorder,- This category describes that which occurs in response to a major life stressor or crisis.

* Bipolar - This type includes both high and low mood swings, as well as a variety of other significant symptoms not present in other forms of the disease.

Other Types of Depressive Categories:

* Post Partum - Major depressive episode that occurs after having a baby. Depressive symptoms usually begin within four weeks of giving birth and can vary in intensity and duration.

* Seasonal Affective Disorder (SAD) - A type of depressive disorder which is characterized by episodes of a major case which reoccur at a specific time of the year (e.g. fall, winter). In the past two years, depressive periods occur at least two times without any episodes that occur at a different time.

* Anxiety - Not an official type (as defined by the DSM). However, anxiety often also occurs with depression. In this case, a depressed individual may also experience anxiety symptoms (e.g. panic attacks) or an anxiety disorder (e.g. PTSD, panic disorder, social phobia, generalized anxiety disorder).

* Chronic - Major depressive episode that lasts for at least two years.

* Double - Someone who has Dysthymia (chronic mild) and also experiences a major depressive episode (more severe depressive symptoms lasting at least two weeks).

* Endogenous - Endogenous means from within the body. This type is defined as feeling depressed for no apparent reason.

* Situational or Reactive (also known as Adjustment Disorder with Depressed Mood) - Depressive symptoms developing in response to a specific stressful situation or event (e.g. job loss, relationship ending). These symptoms occur within 3 months of the stressor and lasts no longer than 6 months after the stressor (or its consequences) has ended. Depression symptoms cause significant distress or impairs usual functioning (e.g. relationships, work, school) and do not meet the criteria for major depressive disorder.

* Agitated - Kind of major depressive disorder which is characterized by agitation such as physical and emotional restlessness, irritability and insomnia, which is the opposite of many depressed individuals who have low energy and feel slowed down physically and mentally.

* Psychotic - Major depressive episode with psychotic symptoms such as hallucinations (e.g. hearing voices), delusions (false beliefs).

* Atypical (Sub-type of Major or Dysthymia) - Characterized by a temporary improvement in mood in

reaction to positive events and two (or more) of the following: o significant weight gain or increase in appetite

o over sleeping

o heavy feeling in arms or legs

o long standing pattern of sensitivity to rejection

* Melancholic (Sub-type of Major Depressive Disorder) - Main features of this kind of depression include either a loss of pleasure in virtually all activities or mood does not temporarily improve in response to a positive event. Also, three (or more) of the following are present:

o Depressed mood that has a distinct quality (e.g. different from feeling depressed when grieving)

o Depressive feeling is consistently worse in the morning

o Waking up earlier than usual (at last 2 hours)

o Noticeable excessive movement or slowing down

o Significant decrease in appetite or weight loss

o Feeling excessive or inappropriate guilt

*Catatonic - (Sub-type of Major Depressive Disorder) - This type is characterized by at least two of the following:

o Loss of voluntary movement and inability to react to one's environment

o Excessive movement (purposeless and not in response to one's environment)

o Extreme resistance to instructions/suggestions or unable/unwilling to speak

o Odd or inappropriate voluntary movements or postures (e.g. repetitive movements, bizarre mannerisms or facial expressions)

o Involuntarily repeating someone's words or movements in a meaningless way Treatment will differ depending on the type of depression based on its severity and various symptoms.

For example, the focus of therapy may vary or different antidepressants may be prescribed targeting certain symptoms. Common factors can lead to different types. Substance abuse can lead to depressive disorder. Both alcoholics and drug abusers can contract it. Mental disorder historically has a stigma associated with it. Prior to mental illness being recognized as a disease it was considered by many to be a personal defect. As a result treatment wasn't applied in a way that could help the patient. Negative effects persist through all the stages of depression. Therefore treatment requires early detection.

Major depressive disorder is probably one of the most common forms. You probably know a handful of people who suffer from it. The sufferer seems to walk around with the weight of the world on his or her shoulders. He or she seems disinterested in becoming involved in regular activities and seems convinced that he or she will always be in this hopeless state. There is a lack of interest in sexual activity and in appetite and a weight loss.

TYPES

Atypical: is a variation that is slightly different from it's major variety. The sufferer is sometimes able to experience happiness and moments of elation. Symptoms of the atypical type include fatigue, oversleeping, overeating and weight gain. People who suffer from it believe that outside events control their mood (i.e. success, attention and praise). Episodes can last for months or a sufferer may live with it forever.

Psychotic: sufferers begin to hear and see imaginary things - - sounds, voices and visuals that do not exist. These are referred to as hallucinations, which are generally more common with someone suffering from schizophrenia. The hallucinations are not "positive" like they are with a manic depressive. The sufferer imagines frightening and negative sounds and images. Dysthymia: Many people just walk around seeming depressed - - simply sad, blue or melancholic. They have been this way all of their lives. This is dysthymia - - a condition that people are not even aware of but just live with daily. They go through life feeling unimportant, dissatisfied, frightened and simply don't enjoy their lives. Medication is beneficial for this type.

Manic: can be defined as an emotional disorder characterized by changing mood shifts can sometimes be quite rapid. People who suffer from manic depressive disorder have an extremely high rate of suicide.

Seasonal:, which medical professionals call seasonal affective disorder, or SAD, is something that occurs only at a certain time of the year, usually winter. It is sometimes called "winter blues." Although it is predictable, it can be very severe.

Cyclothymic Disorder:A milder yet more enduring type of bipolar disorder. A person's mood alternates between a less severe mania (known as hypomania) and a less severe case.

Mood Disorder, due to a General Medical Condition caused or precipitated by a known or unknown physical medical condition such as hypothyroidism.)

Substance Induced Mood Disorder may be caused or precipitated by the use or abuse of substances such as drugs, alcohol, medications, or toxins.

Seasonal Affective Disorder (SAD):This condition affects people during specific times or seasons of the year. During the winter months individuals feel depressed and lethargic, but during other months their moods may be normal.

Postpartum:A rare form occurring in women within approximately one week to six months after giving birth to a child.

Premenstrual Dysphoric Disorder:This is an uncommon type of depressive disorder affecting a small percentage of menstruating women. It is a cyclical condition in which women may feel depressed and irritable for one or two weeks before their menstrual period each month.

What exactly is a depressive disorder?

Depressive disorders have been with mankind since the beginning of recorded history. In the Bible, King David, as well as Job, suffered from this affliction. Hippocrates referred to it as melancholia, which literally means black bile. Black bile, along with blood, phlegm, and yellow bile were the four humors (fluids) that described the basic medical physiology theory of that time. It is also referred to as clinical depression, has been portrayed in literature and the arts for hundreds of years, but what do we mean today when we refer to a depressive disorder? In the 19th century, it was seen as an inherited weakness of temperament. In the first half of the 20th century, Freud linked the development of depressive feelings to guilt and conflict. John Cheever, the author and a modern sufferer of depressive disorder, wrote of conflict and experiences with his parents as influencing his development of the disease.

The symptoms that help a doctor identify the disorder include:

* constant feelings of sadness, irritability, or tension

* decreased interest or pleasure in usual activities or hobbies

* loss of energy, feeling tired despite lack of activity

* a change in appetite, with significant weight loss or weight gain

* a change in sleeping patterns, such as difficulty sleeping, early morning awakening, or sleeping too much

* restlessness or feeling slowed down

* decreased ability to make decisions or concentrate

* feelings of worthlessness, hopelessness, or guilt

* thoughts of suicide or death

If you are experiencing any or several of these symptoms, you should talk to your doctor about whether you are suffering. From chronic illnesses such as heart disease to pain perception, sex, and sleep.

Sexual Problems - Learn how medicines can affect sexual desire and sexual performance.

Sleep Problems - Find out how this disease disturbs sleep and get some effective tips to help your sleep problems. Warning Signs

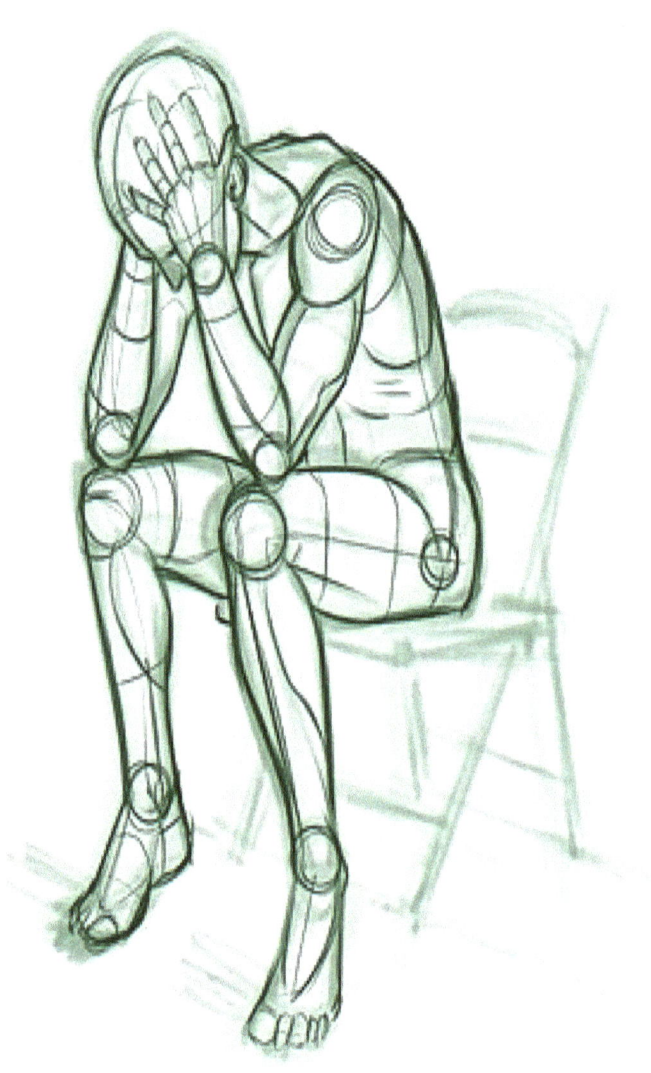

CHAPTER 5
SIGNS OF DEPRESSION

The symptoms of depression are often subtle at first. The two most significant symptoms of depression are Sadness or Hopelessness. However there are other symptoms of depression. Recognizing the symptoms of depression is usually the toughest part and is critical to the treatment of depression. Take a look at the following symptoms of depression below.

Signs, Signs Everywhere Signs and Symptoms of Depression.

It's critical to understand the early warning signs of depression so that you can recognize them and get the treatment you deserve. Everybody's symptoms of depression show up in different ways and in different degrees of those symptoms, but usually, they're severe enough to mess up your everyday life.

First realize that in order to be classified as depression, symptoms must persist for at least two weeks. So what are the symptoms?

Well here's a list:

-Persistent sadness or unhappiness

-Lethargy

-Loss of interest in previously enjoyable activities

-Irritability

-Sudden change in appetite

-Disruption of normal sleep pattern

-Physical discomfort

-Difficulty thinking or concentrating

-Thoughts of suicide or death

-Anxious, numb, or "empty" mood

-Feelings of worthlessness

-Helplessness

-Guilt

-Feelings of hopelessness

-Pessimism

-Insomnia

-Early-morning awakening

-Oversleeping

-Decreased energy

-Increased appetite with weight gain

-Decreased appetite with weight loss

-Thoughts of self-injury

-Persistent physical symptoms that do not respond to treatment, such as headaches, backaches, etc.

CHAPTER 6
CAUSES OF DEPRESSION

Nearly everyone experiences occasional feelings of sadness; depressed feelings are a natural reaction to disappointment, loss, difficulties in life, or low self-esteem. But when periods of intense sadness last for weeks at a time and hamper your ability to function normally, you may be suffering from clinical, or major, depression.

Depression is a complex disorder which can be caused by many different agents; mental health experts believe that major depression is actually a symptom of one or more underlying health issues, rather than an isolated disease. Understanding why you are experiencing depression can help your mental health care provider direct your treatment appropriately, enabling you to enjoy renewed quality of life.

* Causes of Depression

The health conditions and genetic/environmental factors discussed here are all known to be associated with depression. Determining precisely why you are feeling depressed and addressing the particular issue are critical to solving your depression problem and allowing you to live to your fullest potential.

- Genetics

As with numerous other health disorders, it is clear that heredity plays a role in depression. Not everyone who has depressive symptoms has a family history of emotional issues; nor does having depression in your family guarantee that you will experience depression. However, research has shown that individuals with mental illness in their background have a greater chance of experiencing symptoms of depression themselves.

- Trauma & Stress

Traumatic and stressful life events, such as loss of a loved one, abuse, chronic illness or pain, or a move to an unfamiliar location can trigger depression in certain individuals. These events result in changes in neurotransmitter levels (discussed later in more detail), leading to brain chemistry imbalances that cause depression symptoms.

- Medications & Recreational Drugs

There are a large number of substances which many of us use regularly that can cause depression in some people. Prescription medications, birth control pills, anti-inflammatory drugs (including steroids), antihistamines, cholesterol pills, high blood pressure medications, antidepressants and tranquilizers are all linked to depressive symptoms. Nicotine, caffeine, alcohol, and street drugs are all known to lead to depression in certain individuals, as well.

- Neurotransmitter Imbalances & Abnormalities in Brain Physiology

Neurotransmitters are chemical "messengers" in the brain that regulate mood, thought, and memory. When neurotransmitters are not available at sufficient levels, depression can be the result.

Researchers have noted that individuals with depression often have an abnormally small hippocampus, a small structure in the brain that is closely associated with memory. A smaller hippocampus has fewer serotonin receptors; serotonin is a neurotransmitter that is vital in regulating emotions.

- Brain Inflammation

Inflammation, often present with autoimmune disorders such as diabetes, triggers the body's immune system response. Regulatory proteins called cytokines are marshaled into action to fight off possible infection; these peptides create a stress response, altering the levels of certain neurotransmitters, which results in depressive symptoms.

- Toxicity

Environmental toxins, such as heavy metals and molds, can trigger an immune reaction which sets off a cytokine response.

- Digestive Disorders

Digestive dysfunction, including bowel disorders, yeast overgrowth, gluten and other food allergies, and impaired digestion of proteins, can also set off an immune system response which can lead to depression.

- Nutritional Imbalances

Many important nutrients, especially the B vitamins, minerals such as zinc and magnesium, and the Omega 3 fatty acids, are building blocks for important neurotransmitters. Insufficient dietary intake of these nutrients can result in neurotransmitter imbalances, a significant cause of depression symptoms.

- Impaired Methylation

Methylation, a metabolic process which takes place in every cell in the body, is important for the manufacture of hormones, the regulation of neurotransmitters, and the synchronization of the neural networks that affect mood and cognition. When this process is impaired, it can disrupt the entire system.

-Hormone Imbalances

When hormones such as insulin, thyroid or adrenal hormone, and sex hormones are not available at proper levels, they can negatively affect the way we think and feel.

Depression is a serious illness which can have a significant negative impact on your life. Fortunately, lab testing is available that can help you to pinpoint the exact cause of your depression, allowing your health care provider to assist you in choosing the best treatment for your depressive symptoms. With proper care, your symptoms should disappear, leaving you to enjoy life to its fullest once again.

CHAPTER 7

63 IDEAS TO GET RID OF DEPRESSION

No matter what kind of depression you have, the pain is the same-caused by a chemical imbalance in your brain. No matter what you're depressed about, or even if you don't know why you're depressed, there are some simple things you can do to reduce your pain and anxiety, and get yourself feeling better.

Simple cognitive behavior techniques and exercises can lessen pain and stimulate more productive thinking. Low-key physical and mental activity can also speed recovery.

1. Relax your shoulders, take a deep breath and don't panic! Millions of perfectly normal people have struggled with all kinds of depression and learned how to get out of it. You are not alone. You have options.

2. First, why do you feel so bad? It's not because of your problems. It's because of your brain chemistry. There are two main parts of the brain, the thinking part (the neocortex) and the emotional part (the subcortex). When you're depressed, your subcortex is reacting to stress chemicals, and producing excruciating pain and panic.

3. To add to your misery, your subcortex sucks up additional neural energy from the neocortex until it is practically non-functioning. So you can't think straight, plus you're in agony.

4. You feel helpless, but there's a lot you can do. Your body is experiencing a perfectly normal reaction to the over-supply of stress chemicals in your brain.

5. You need to reduce the neural energy in the subcortex and re-power the neocortex. You can do this with cognitive behavioral mind techniques that will spark up neural activity in the neocortex. With a little practice you will be able to do this any time depression hits you. A few facts about how your brain works will also help you cope.

6. Your first task is to free yourself from the kinds of negative and downer thoughts that power the subcortex and support the pain of your depression. Get rid of thoughts like:

- 'I'm depressed'
- 'I feel terrible'
- 'What's the use'
- 'I can't stand this pain anymore'

7. Switch your Thoughts! To get rid of any depressive thoughts, simply switch out of thinking them. Since the brain is basically a 'yes brain,' it's hard to not think something. The way to not think a negative or depressive thought is to think another thought instead of it.

8. The best way to think another thought instead of a depressive thought is to use the simple cognitive behavioral technique called 'brainswitching.'

Choose any neutral or nonsense thought, in advance, to have 'at the ready' to substitute for any depressive thought that pops up. When you're depressed, you're in too much pain to think one up.

- Make it a thought that will not stimulate any negative emotional association. It could be
- a silly song or rhyme fragment like 'Row, row, row your boat'
- a mantra like 'Om Padme'
- a neutral or nonsense word like 'hippity-hop, 'green frog,' or 'yadda yadda'
- a prayer like the 23rd Psalm.

9. It may seem silly to suggest that saying 'green frog' over and over to yourself can get rid of depression, but there's a scientific reason for the exercise. Thinking a neutral or nonsense thought interrupts the depressive thought pattern and weakens it. How? See #10.

10. The brain always follows the direction of its most current dominant thought. When you make your neutral or nonsense thought dominant by thinking it over and over repetitively, it automatically kicks the depressive thought out of its dominant position and the brain ceases tracking it so actively. It turns toward the neutral thought.

11. Brainswitching will automatically increase neural activity in the neocortex, and reduce neural activity in the subcortex. It will continually interrupt the message that you are depressed from one part

of the brain to the other.

12. Brainswitching distracts your attention from your emotional brain and directs it to the thinking part of the brain. Depression only happens in the subcortex. There's never any depression in the neocortex.

13. You can brainswitch for a few seconds the first time you try it. With practice you can do it longer. You may be surprised to know that, even in the worst depression, your neocortex always remains calm and immediately available to you. And you can always brainswitch to it.

14. Keep choosing your neutral thought again when you lose concentration. You must actually do this exercise to activate the neocortex. It's not just an idea. Ideas don't work for depression. Only behavior works. A thought is just a thought but thinking a thought over and over again is behavior!

15. Always brainswitch to break the continuity of depression's grip on you. Depression, like any other anxious emotion or feeling, can't maintain itself unless you think it repetitively. Think something else instead-like 'green frog.'

16. Do not think a depressive thought twice. No depressive thought can, by itself, turn into depression if you continually refuse to think it. A depressive thought is over as quick as any other thought. Don't choose to think it again. Depression hits you with a first thought but you can refuse to think the second thought. For depression to 'take hold,' you must continuously think it.

17. Move into Action! Always brainswitch whenever a depressive or stressful thought threatens to ' take over.' An unhappy thought is just a thought. It can pop into your mind at any moment. It is an event that happens to you. Choosing to think an unhappy, anxious or depressive thought over and over is behavior. It is something that you do and you can learn not to do it.

18. Be aware of the 'early warning' sad or negative feelings that usually precede a full-blown depressive episode. Confront your depression right away. 'Okay I know what this is. This is depression coming. I have to side-step it with a neutral thought.'

19. Get out of depression at earlier stages by checking out the passive thinking that happens when you just let your mind wander. Passive thinking can often 'go negative' on you. When it does, switch to on-purpose thinking before negative thinking becomes dominant in your brain. The way you do 'on-purpose' thinking is to choose a specific thought to think, or by deciding to do some task which then directs your thinking in line with the task at hand.

20. Pry yourself loose from being fused with the pain of your depression before you disappear into it.

Find a small thinking space between you and your pain. Yes, you feel agonized and hopeless, but you can also focus slightly aside from your agony and hopelessness. You are not hopeless, you are the observer of your feeling of hopelessness. Accept some discomfort in a more detached way. Depression is a horrible feeling. It is not you! YOU are you! You are not a feeling. You are a person who is having a feeling.

21. Focus your mind on some low-key physical action:

• Brush your teeth.

• Clean your desk.

• Swing your arms in circles.

• Jog, or take a walk, and keep on walking until you feel tired.

• Smile! -not because you're happy, but to relax your tense face muscles.

22. Get yourself up and going with any kind of moving-around exercises. The more you move into physical action, the less depression has a chance to settle in on you. Put on some music, dance around the room. Not because you will feel like dancing, but because depression hates you to dance. Do something your depression hates.

23. Distract yourself from the pain of depression with small chores. Do them while thinking your neutral or nonsense thought. Do your chore. Think your thought. Ignore your depression by thinking objectively about what you are doing not subjectively about how you are feeling. Your stress and pain will begin to lessen.

24. Look around you if you can't think of any chores to do. There is always some 'next thing' that can distract you from your pain. Any outward-focused action can help you turn away from self-focus on the pain of your depression. Take out the trash.

25. Do the 'next thing' when paralyzed by fear or depression. Life never abandons us without giving us the 'next thing' to do. It is security for our sanity and for the healing power of positive behavior. The next thing may just be to take a shower.

26. After the first task, the second task will become even more obvious. Do what you decide to do, not what you feel like doing. Depression never deprives you of 'will,' only motivation. You won't want to do anything, but you can do it.

27. Focus on Behavior, Not Feelings! Since depression kills motivation, use your 'neutral thought' exercise as if it is a motivation pill. Quick! Slip a neutral thought in on your depressive thought.

28. Decide ahead of time to do your exercise anyway, even though you feel like it won't work. Anticipate the fact that depression always robs you of all hope, including hope that any exercise will work.

29. Behavior always trumps feelings. But for a trump to win, you have to play it. No fearful or depressive feeling is powerful enough to prevent you from engaging your body in some kind of mental or physical behavior. You just need to stand up to your fearful feelings and show them 'who's boss.' Behavior is boss.

- No fearful or depressive feeling can rise up and conquer you. It must frighten you into surrendering.

- Feelings are just your own neural patterns twanging for attention.

- Accept fearful feelings; move forward with positive behavior.

- When you accept fearful feelings, they finish and die. Fear feeds them and keeps them alive

- Feelings cannot be more powerful than you are--behavior rules!

30. Depression is not something that you are, it is something you do and you can learn not to do it. Depression is a terrible feeling. Feelings are very powerful but they are not intelligent. They can be wrong. You don't have to do feelings. You can change the thinking that caused the feelings and then the feelings will change to reflect the new thoughts. On-purpose thought always trumps passive or automatic thought.

31. On-purpose thought is always more current than passive thought, so automatically it's more dominant than passive thought. Your brain always follows the direction of its most current dominant thought. If your depression patterns are well-imprinted from practicing them, don't worry. Practicing new thinking forms new brain patterns without depression. You can use the new get-out-of-depression patterns instead of the old get-into-depression ones.

32. During depression, the physical pain, the psychological fear, the feelings of worthlessness, helplessness, and despair, are all bound up and entangled in a neural pattern that takes on a life of its

own, seemingly independent of our will. The key here is seemingly. We are not usually aware that we focus our attention away from our will when we're depressed. We focus only on the depressive pattern. We can focus on our behavior instead.

33. Decide to concentrate on something--a book or some work. Depression doesn't prevent you from concentrating. That's a myth. Depression makes you forget that you are already concentrating on something-on depression! Don't let depression interrupt work. Let work interrupt your depression.

34. Whenever depression interrupts your concentration, interrupt it back! You have one attention only. If you are thinking a neutral, nonsense, rational, or productive thought, you cannot, at the same instant, be thinking a depressive thought.

35. Pay attention to your self-talk. It will indicate what kind of thinking you're doing-passive or on-purpose, self-focused or outer-focused, subjective (about your feelings) or objective (about other things). Self-talk is that on-going conversation you have with yourself in your own mind that you usually don't pay any attention to.

36. Don't Forget-Your Mind is Tricking You! Your mind tricks you into anxious thinking via unnoticed self-talk. Trick it back! Replace negative self-talk. If you hit a red light, self-talk might be 'I'm going to be late!' Change to 'Relax, I'll be fine.'

37. You think you're depressed because of your problems. This is a mind trick. You're always depressed because of your depression. It's the chemistry! Anxious thoughts trigger the fight-or-flight response that produces stress chemicals, causing a chemical imbalance in your brain.

38. It seems your whole self is depressed. This is a mind trick. Depression only occurs in the subcortex. There's never any depression in the thinking part of the brain.

39. Depression seems like present reality. This is a mind trick. Depression is a feeling, already past, which you must then replay (rethink) in memory 'as if' it is present reality. This is due to the instantaneous process of 'pain perception.' To experience any feeling of physical pain or emotion (which is always produced in the subcortex) we must first think (acknowledge) the feeling in the neocortex-after we have it.

Cases are recorded of athletes who break a bone during a game and don't experience any pain until the game is over. Neocortical concentration on the game blocked pain signals sent to the neocortex that should have alerted them to the pain of their injury.

40. Depression is the opposite of living in the NOW. Thinking how you feel is past feeling re-played in thinking 'as if' it's present. The process of experiencing a past feeling as if it's a present happening is beneath our level of awareness but once we are aware of it, we can slip a quick neutral thought in on our depression and weaken it.

41. There's a huge difference between self-focus and self-awareness. Self-focus is thinking about how you feel, and it is never connected to present reality. Self-awareness is connecting with present reality by getting outer-focused. When you find yourself self-focused, get outer-focused as soon as possible with physical or objective mental activity that connects you to the neocortex. Self-focus is the opposite of living in the NOW because self-focus is thinking about your feelings which are always 'past.'

42. To get out of self-focus and connect to present reality, think objective thoughts about the people or the physical things around you. Think about or talk to another person. Objective thinking can immediately help detach you from the subjective thinking of the pain of your depression. It also helps when you feel self-conscious, socially stressed and alienated.

43. This is really tricky. If you feel bad, you have unwittingly instructed your brain to feel bad. The brain works by learned association (think 'salt,' the thought 'pepper' automatically fires up). A negative thought is instructions to your brain to fire up other similar negative thoughts in its memory bank. If you think 'sad' then similar 'downer' thoughts like 'depressed' will pop up, or 'worthless' or ' I feel terrible.'

44. When you think any thought at all, that thought becomes a specific instruction to your brain because it works by learned association. Your brain will pick up the thought like a football, and connect it with the other similar thoughts stored in its memory banks. Think 'green frog' not 'sad.'

45. Use 'learned association' to get out of depression the same way you got in it. Neutral thoughts spark up other neutral thoughts and your brain moves from depressive thinking to neutral thinking.

46. Get the 'process of positivity' working for you in your brain. The inherent importance of any small victory is not relevant. The process of being positive is more important than the content.

47. Even if you over-ate there might be some small thing you passed up. 'Hey, I didn't eat that third brownie. I was victorious over the third brownie.' Our small triumphs don't need to make sense in the 'real world.' They just need to be positive so that they will stimulate positive thinking in our mind by

learned association.

48. Re-engage! Your depression wants you to isolate yourself and keep yourself stressed. Fight back! Re-engage with other people or things-go to the movies, read biographies in the library, take a long walk downtown.

49. Question your thoughts. It is helpful to think this, or is it unhelpful? Is it helpful to believe this, or is it unhelpful? Unhelpful thoughts should never be an option. No thought can make you think it. You have the power to not think any thought. In order to not think a thought, simply think another thought instead of it-like 'hippity hop.'

50. Don't call yourself names like 'I'm Depressed' or 'I'm Bipolar.' Labels of illness like 'I'm bipolar' don't contribute to wellbeing. Cancer patients feel better who tell themselves that they are 'doing better,' rather than thinking, 'I have cancer.' Treat

these names like any negative thought.

51. See your problems in context of time, a week out of your lifespan; in terms of help that might be available from family or friends; in terms of developing character from the experience of your failure.

52. Carry a paperback joke book. When depression threatens, read the book for at least five minutes. Depression will not want you to do this. Do it anyway.

53. Laugh out loud for two minutes. The brain doesn't know the difference between being happy and pretending to be happy. Happy thoughts produce happy feelings. The feelings are genuine though the thoughts that generated them were fake.

54. Put off depression as long as you can. 'It's coming, but I'll do my exercises first before it's all the way here.' Or, 'I'll check my email first.' This way you interrupt the direct neural pathway to depression, and the brain can 'forget' it was heading for depression.

55. To produce calm thinking, force neutral thoughts on your brain as you would force exercise on your body. This imprints in your memory bank a usable neural pattern that you can access whenever depression attacks. If you want to be happy, you have to first get your brain to do happy.

56. Allow space for your panicky feelings. They are very scary, but they are just normal reactions to

stress chemicals that are the same in every human body. It might be difficult to breathe or swallow, your heart might start racing, you might get the shakes or the sweats, feel like you're going to die! Let your feelings be where they are, while you temporarily focus your attention on some deep breathing. Just easy. Just easy. Breathing doesn't have to be perfect. Just easy. Watch your breath coming in, and watch it going out. In and out.

57. Depression is not real life. It's a panic room of the mind. Get back out of your panic room into real life again.

58. You're responsible for your mind, not to your mind (as if it were in charge of you.) You should be in charge of your mind, so it does what you want. You should direct your thinking, not collapse into it; manage moods cognitively, not obey them.

59. Do not re-think old horror stories. Say to yourself. 'I will not go there.' How you don't go there is head elsewhere in your mind. Your brain can't follow two chains of thought going in two directions at once. It will follow your current dominant thought.

60. It's possible to choose to live by the precept that you will accept no other option than going forward with your day in some productive manner, no matter how humble, no matter how desperate you feel.

61. There's the power of positive thinking. There's also the power of positive doing! When you get depressed, do something physically and mentally active. Re-engage your attention in any objective thinking or outer-focus, and get yourself out of dangerous subjective self-focus.

62. Thoughts are not reality. They are tools to help you through your day. Choose the right tools. If you think good thoughts you will have good feelings, you will see good in others, and in yourself, and you'll see good things in your path.

63. You can't always decide to be happy. You can always decide to be cheerful. Happiness is a feeling. Cheerfulness is on-purpose, rational behavior. Being cheerful ultimately makes you happy.

CONCLUSION

Scientific studies show that people who feel they have no control over their life are more prone to depression, but people who feel they have control over their life in general are happy and positive.

Therefore we can say in a generality that a feeling of lack of control leads to depression.

We liken the mind to the tires of a car, in that a poor quality tire gives a very poor ability to control the car, it will not be stable to drive with an off balance wobbly or flat tire. If your mind is not strong and stable enough, you will feel you have no control over events and thus the future of your life, which makes life hopeless and will lead you to depression.

Let's look a this process in reverse. If you feel a sense of depression or hopelessness in your life, we can say that a cause of this is that you do not feel you have control over the events in your life, over what will happen to you and over what you will do. By exercising control over your life, by making decisions, you will alleviate the feeling of hopelessness and depression.

Control is the master key. In the car, by changing the tires to a higher quality, you will have better control. In the mind it is a matter of the quality of your thoughts. By changing the quality of your thoughts to more powerful, positive and decisive, you will alter your level of control over the events in your life and cure the problem that way.

This is actually the easiest thing in the world to do, because it is as simple as taking action, by making a decision.

If you acknowledge that depression is caused by a feeling of lack of control, and that the mind is the weak point between you and the world, meaning who is in control; you the driver or the wobbly tires reacting to the bumps in the road sending you into a ravine. If we change the tires, meaning the type and quality of your thoughts through your actions, you will gain strength of character, will-power and confidence.

To do this it is important to accept that the outcome of the decision is irrelevant at this point in the process of taking control. The point is that you make a decision. That you decide and take control and implement action by making a decision, the outcome is irrelevant because the quality of the mind is that you choose, you are in control of the decision.

Using the example of dating, since loneliness is a major cause of depression as well, if you take the action, make a decision and speak to that person on the street or in the cafe who you find attractive, the power of the decision to take action is very exhilarating as long as you are not concerned with the outcome.

Only by taking control and learning from your experiences will you be able to improve the quality of your decisions. It is the same as when you start working and do not have much money, you have to buy less expensive tires, but as you improve and make more money, you can buy better quality tires and a car.

In the same way, you make decisions and take control of your life and as you do, over time, the quality of your decisions improve thus giving you greater power. Unless you are willing to accept that the outcome of the decision is irrelevant, but the point is that you made a decision, then you will never take control of your life because you are too scared to make a wrong decision, and thus remain depressed.

People who turn all their affairs over to God, submitting to the will of God, that everything is in God's hands, have relinquished control, and are thus now helpless. In fact, what they have done is avoid responsibility for their life.

'God helps those who help themselves.' This very well known saying is always forgotten by people of blind faith, who normally are very poor, depressed and find their only comfort in brainwashing themselves with the thought that God knows best.

There is a good story about the civil defense evacuating people from an approaching tornado. Some people stood fast refusing to leave with the explanation that God will protect them. Who do you think is sending the tornado!!!

This is the self destructive foolishness of blind faith. Blind faith is not just in religion, it is in following anyone you trust without thinking for yourself, be that a parent, teacher or employer.

Take responsibility for your life, have faith in the one being which has direct control over your life, YOU.

Success comes to those who DARE and ACT!

www.ingramcontent.com/pod-product-compliance
Lightning Source LLC
Chambersburg PA
CBHW061148010526

44118CB00026B/2907